THE ACA LEGAL SERIES

Volume 3

"Law and Management of a Counseling Agency or Private Practice"

THE ACA LEGAL SERIES

Series Editor: Theodore P. Remley, Jr., JD, PhD

Volume 1   ***Preparing for Court Appearances***
Theodore P. Remley, Jr., JD, PhD

Volume 2   ***Documentation in Counseling Records***
Robert W. Mitchell, ACSW

Volume 3   ***Law and Management of a Counseling Agency or Private Practice***
Ronald K. Bullis, MDiv, JD

Volume 4   ***Counseling Minor Clients***
Mark M. Salo, MEd
Stephen G. Shumate, JD, MS

Volume 5   ***The Counselor as Expert Witness***
William J. Weikel, PhD
Paula Richardson Hughes, JD

Volume 6   ***Confidentiality and Privileged Communication***
Gibbs L. Arthur, Jr., MEd
Carl D. Swanson, JD, EdD

Volume 7   ***Legal Issues in Marriage and Family Counseling***
Patricia Stevens-Smith, PhD
Marcia M. Hughes, JD

THE ACA LEGAL SERIES
Volume 3

"Law and Management of a Counseling Agency or Private Practice"

Ronald K. Bullis, MDiv, JD

Series Editor
Theodore P. Remley, Jr., JD, PhD

Copyright © 1993 by the American Counseling Association

All rights reserved.

American Counseling Association
5999 Stevenson Avenue
Alexandria, VA 22304

Cover design by Sarah Jane Valdez

Library of Congress Cataloging-in-Publication Data

Bullis, Ronald K.
    Law and management of a counseling agency or private practice /
by Ronald K. Bullis.
    p. cm.
    Includes bibliographical references.
    ISBN 1-55620-101-X
    1. Counselors—Legal status, laws, etc.—United States.
2. Counseling—Law and legislation—United States. 3. Counseling—
United States. I. Title.
  KF2910.P75B85 1993
  344.73'044—dc20
  [347.30444]   92-20722
  ISSN 1064-2226   CIP

The ACA Legal Series, Volume 3

Printed in the United States of America

To Amy
my bride and my blessing

Contents

Biographies ix
Preface 1
Glossary 3
Contracts 7
Advertising 15
Copyright 19
Employment Discrimination 25
Sexual Harassment 33
Employer Vicarious Liability 39
Agency 45
Insurance 49
Legal Audits 53
Frequently Asked Questions 59
Guidelines for Practice 63
Summary 67
Discussion Questions 69
Suggested Readings 71
References 73

Biographies

Ronald K. Bullis is an ethicist and counselor specializing in the law and decision-making processes of professions and professionals, particularly as they relate to diverse cultures. He holds a JD degree from Syracuse University College of Law and a master of divinity degree from Princeton Theological Seminary and is a PhD candidate in clinical social work. He is also a licensed professional counselor in Virginia and an ordained Presbyterian minister. He is currently at work on books addressing the legal and ethical issues arising from sexual misconduct and other dual relations between professionals and clients as well as a book addressing the legal issues in pastoral care and counseling. He is a past president of the Fort Berthold Community College on the Fort Berthold Indian Reservation in North Dakota and has taught law and religion at Virginia Union University in Richmond and at Princeton Theological Seminary.

Theodore P. Remley, Jr., Series Editor, is Executive Director of the American Counseling Association. Immediately prior to assuming this position, Dr. Remley was chair of the Department of Counselor Education at Mississippi State University in Starkville. He holds a PhD from the Department of Counselor Education at the University of Florida in Gainesville and a JD in law from the Catholic University of America in Washington, DC.

Preface

This monograph continues The ACA Legal Series designed to address legal issues confronted by counselors, therapists, social workers, and other mental health professionals. It examines relatively new areas of legal liability for mental health professionals. These areas arise from legal theories that increasingly hold employers liable for a large number of actions by both the employers themselves and employees. Without notice and knowledge of these legal theories and concomitant liability, employers and employees alike risk a wide range of civil and criminal penalties.

Addressed in this monograph are laws that govern the business and management of mental health practices. Consider, for example, cases in which both the counselor and the counselor's employing agency or counseling center are sued for a professional negligence (malpractice) action alleging wrongdoing by the counselor alone. Under several theories of liability, the employing agency as well as supervisors themselves may be sued for alleged harm done by employees.

The rationale for this monograph is that state and federal laws regulate counseling agencies as well as counselors who are part of a private practice. Both state and federal laws have placed restrictions and limitations upon the mental health and counseling industries just as they have upon other industries. Mental health practitioners who consider themselves exempt or immune from industry and corporate regulation place themselves, their supervisors, and their business in legal jeopardy.

This publication is seeded liberally with law cases. Such cases give meat and muscle to the skeleton of legal principles and serve to illustrate points of law with specific examples. In addition, such cases dramatically demonstrate the fact that law is applied to situations with which the reader might readily identify. Although the case results may differ from state to state, the mental health professional can see examples of how such events and circumstances are resolved in court. Thus, law cases can provide pointed object lessons. It is hoped that they also provide the "ounce of prevention" necessary to avoid litigation and harm to the public.

Three warnings need expression:

1. It should be specifically and emphatically stated that this publication is intended only to raise legal issues, not to offer legal advice. This publication, although helpful for mental health professionals, supervisors, and their employers, cannot replace competent legal counsel. Readers are urged to get such counsel.
2. This monograph concentrates on federal law. Because state laws may differ widely, making a close examination of each state's law is impossible. Readers should note, therefore, that state law should be consulted on each of the topics examined in this volume.
3. This monograph does not exhaust the issues and information on any topic. Such examinations would each require their own books—and thick ones at that! Instead, this volume offers a basic understanding of the issues involved, and is intended to sensitize the human development professional to those issues, in order to help prevent claims and lawsuits.

The format of this publication is designed to be "counselor friendly." Each substantive area of the law—contracts, advertising, copyright, employment discrimination (including sex discrimination, pregnancy discrimination, and the Americans With Disabilities Act), sexual harassment, employer liability, agency, and insurance—has its own section. The final substantive section consists of suggestions for counselor legal protection through "legal audits."

Glossary

Agency: When one person acts with the authority of another. This relationship is often described in law in terms of either master and servant or principal and agent. The law of agency addresses issues of legal responsibility of the master for the wrongful acts of employees. (See Vicarious Employer Liability.)

Burden of Proof: The level of burden legally required to win a case. For criminal trials the burden lies with the prosecutor to convict *beyond a reasonable doubt*. The lesser burdens of *clear and convincing* and *preponderance of the evidence* are reserved for civil trials.

Civil Law: Law that governs behavior among private parties. Civil law includes the law of torts, contracts, and wills. Civil law is often contrasted with criminal law. (See Criminal Law.)

Contract: An agreement creating mutual obligations and privileges. Such an agreement can be either written or oral to be legal, but it must be an agreement between legally competent parties and must have an inducement or cause (legal consideration).

Criminal Law: Law, derived from public officials and legislators, designed to protect the public safety and welfare. Criminal law can be contrasted with civil law. (See Civil Law.)

Damages: The monetary awards given to plaintiffs winning their case. Damages are of several kinds including *compensa-*

tory damages for provable expenses due to injury and *punitive* damages levied to deter others from doing the same wrong.

Defendants: Generally, those who must defend against a legal action.

Deposition: A document, in question-and-answer format and generally made under oath, that solicits information from possible witnesses in a lawsuit. The deposition may be used later in the actual trial.

Discovery: The part of the litigation process in which each side requests pertinent information from the other side. The attorney for each party may request documents, take depositions, or both, to gain access to information that may be used at trial.

Fiduciary: A trust; a legal obligation to act in another's best interest. A fiduciary is one who has taken on an obligation to act honestly and loyally, and for the benefit of another. Courts have held that counseling professionals are fiduciaries of their clients and can be held liable if the counselors breach that trust.

Legal Duty: An obligation imposed by action of law that requires an action or an obligation to refrain from an action.

Liability: The legal determination of responsibility. In civil cases money damages may be the penalty. In criminal cases, either money damages or imprisonment may result.

Negligence: A legal determination of wrongdoing. For a negligence action to succeed, four elements are necessary: a duty, a breach of that duty, damages, and a reasonably close (proximate) link between the breach of duty and the resultant harm.

Plaintiffs: Generally, those who initiate a legal action. In a criminal action, the plaintiffs are the government agency that prosecutes the case. In a civil action, the plaintiffs are often private individuals or corporations as well as governments.

Retained Attorney or Attorney on Retainer: An attorney obligated by contractual relationship with an individual or business to be on call for legal counsel should the need arise. The client in such a relationship makes an up-front payment.

Respondeat Superior: A legal doctrine allowing liability against employers for the harm done by an employee. This doctrine is sometimes known as vicarious employer liability.

Sanction: A penalty, either civil or criminal in nature, imposed for a violation or liability.

Subpoena: A court order requiring someone to appear for deposition or to give court testimony.

Torts: The law of private injury to others. Torts are a class of civil law. The word *tort* itself means twisted; thus, a tort is a twisted act, an act that is damaging or that is harmful.

Vicarious Employer Liability: Legal responsibility assumed by an employer on behalf of an employee. *Respondeat superior*, negligent hiring, negligent supervision, and negligent training are forms of vicarious employer responsibility.

Contracts

The soul of any commercial transaction is the contract. The same is true for the commerce of the mental health industry. Counseling contracts are intended to define specifically the rights and responsibilities of both clinician and client. Without such clearly defined terms of obligation and benefit, neither the counselor nor the client can determine whether his or her legal expectations of the other have been met.

Meeting reasonable, clearly defined expectations is the best prevention for avoiding lawsuits. Unexpressed expectations, unclear promises, and unfulfilled bargains are the causes of most lawsuits. Contracts, fully and mutually understood by all persons involved, are not only good business but also good counseling. In fact, as will be discussed later, contracting can be a potent therapeutic tool.

Contract, in law, is defined by the elements necessary to enforce it. Obviously, anyone can make a contract with anyone to do anything. But not all contracts are legally enforceable. For example, a counselor may contract with an intoxicated client for counseling services every day for one-half hour at a rate of $200.00. Although this contract might be written, notarized, and signed by several credible witnesses, it is unlikely that a court will enforce it. This section describes the elements required of an enforceable contract and looks at specific issues in counseling contracts.

Mental health employers and supervisors need to recognize legally enforceable and legally unenforceable contracts for two reasons. One is that almost every official function of a supervisory position involves the affirmative creation and interpretation of contracts. The writing of every grant, the hiring of every employee, the purchasing of every office machine, and the ordering of all office supplies involve the interpretation of contracts. The second reason is that supervisors and employers need to defend their agency or office from voidable contracts. They must, for example, be able to identify and disavow contracts that are materially misrepresentative, unduly influential, or void as against public policy.

Elements of an Enforceable Contract

There are four principal elements of an enforceable contract (Lieberman & Siedel, 1985), each of which has specific application to mental health practitioners and employers: reaching an agreement, achieving legal consideration, making an agreement consistent with law and public policy, and entering the agreement freely, knowingly, and with capacity.

1. Contracting parties must reach a mutually understood agreement. At first glance, one might say, "How could parties to a contract not mutually understand to what they agree?" The answer is that it is easier than you think to misunderstand the terms of a bargain. For example, suppose a counseling agency employer intends to hire a licensed counselor and says that salary is based upon a share of the profits of the counseling center. This sounds simple enough, but can be fraught with misunderstanding. Who will do the calculating, and how and when will the profits be calculated? If the new counselor wants to take on clients in his or her spare time, will these profits be included in the office profits or his or her own? If the counselor does not bring in a minimum amount of business, can the new counselor's share of the profits be reduced? These are only some of the items that can and should be specified in an employment contract.

2. To be enforceable, a contract must include consideration. In other words, parties to a contract must give up something to get something. Essentially, this means that parties receiving a benefit from the agreement must undergo a legal detriment. That is, they agree to give up a right or perform a service they are not already obligated to perform. For example, there is no consideration in an agreement for a counseling center to pay local

police to protect it against burglary. The local police already have an obligation to protect the counseling center. Such an agreement fails for lack of consideration.

3. Agreements incorporated in an enforceable contract must be consistent with public policy and not offend other laws. For example, courts will not enforce a claim for illegal gambling debts. To enforce such a claim would promote activities that are banned by law.

Consider a contract made between a client and an individual falsely representing himself or herself with mental health credentials: Such a contract *may* be invalidated. The determination is based upon three factors: whether a license is required to perform the contract, whether recovery is barred for those unlicensed, and whether the required license is a regulatory license or a revenue license. A *regulatory license* is licensure for requisite skills, education, or experience. A *revenue license* is a license imposed for the sole purpose of raising government revenue; a peddler's license is an example.

States regulate counselors or counseling either by registering, certifying, or licensing. In registry or certification states, the title of *counselor* (or other such term) is regulated, not the process of counseling itself. Other states define and restrict counseling behaviors. A legal assessment as to whether a license is a regulatory license or a revenue license needs to consider whether the state registers, certifies, or licenses counselors.

4. An enforceable contract involves the necessary trinity of free will, knowledge, and capacity. A contract is valid only if the parties enter into it freely. Conversely, a contract can be invalidated if it was entered into under undue duress or by threat. For example, if a counselor uses intimidation or unfair persuasion to get a client to sign counseling agreements, it is unlikely that a court will enforce them.

Capacity here means the *legal* capacity to enter into a contract. Anyone can sign a piece of paper, but that piece of paper, according to the law, can become an enforceable contract only if the parties possess certain attributes. Those who are intoxicated or mentally ill, those who are convicts or minors, may be prohibited from entering into contracts. Again, an examination of state law is required to define specifically those legally able to contract. A counseling professional should not enter into an agreement with a minor, for example. Instead, the contract should be signed by a minor's parent or legal guardian. Additionally, a counseling professional should not enter into an agreement with a client who is under the influence of drugs or alcohol or who is, for any reason, unable to understand the conditions or consequences of the agreement.

Note that contracts need not be written to be legally binding. Both patterns of behavior and oral agreements can rise to the level of an enforceable contract. For example, if a counselor meets with a client the same day of each week, at the same time, and for the same length of time, and receives the same amount of money for services each week, the law may construe the actions to be a contract. Thus, the counselor cannot claim that the client never paid enough. The behavior by both the client and the counselor creates a contract; an unclear contract is an invitation to lawsuits.

Specific Issues in Counseling Contracts

One of the most perplexing contract problems facing mental health counselors with almost any type of contract is the client who fails to pay or otherwise comply with treatment obligations. Under these conditions, the professional may think his or her only recourse is to terminate the client or to write off the bad debt. These, in fact, are not the only choices. Woody (1989) suggested a number of options including educating the client as to financial obligations, motivating the client to pay, determining a reasonable and appropriate fee, documenting services, and collecting debts.

Educating clients about the amount, timing, and the method of payment is an important therapeutic and legal part of the intake process. Clients have a right to know the extent of the professional's fee, any special charges that might accrue (for reports, additional sessions, interest for late payments) and the method of payment. Clients should be informed about how missed appointments and failure to pay will be handled. This impresses upon clients that they are entering into a serious, professional relationship (like that with a lawyer or physician) and that the counselor expects that his or her time and talents will be compensated.

Motivating a client to pay should be seen as an integral and deliberate part of therapy. To delay confronting clients about late payments is to avoid reality. Why should the professional avoid the reality of late payments when the professional would not hesitate to confront the client with reality in other areas of the client's life? Professionals should not hesitate in speaking honestly and directly about overdue accounts and should encourage the client to do likewise. In addition, regular, systematic billing procedures reinforce the notion that paying professional fees is an obligation that will not vanish because it is unpleasant.

Documenting services rendered is a legal and therapeutic necessity. Documenting all professional services is an art. Woody (1989) suggested counting as professional services those client contacts that (1) rely on the professional's skill or judgment, (2) benefit the client, or (3) create professional ethical, regulatory, or liability issues. This formula is both legally and therapeutically sound. When a client calls purportedly to discuss directions to the professional's office and elevates to a discussion of the client's need to be reassured, the "therapeutic fee clock" should begin ticking and the time documented and billed. Additionally, should the counseling professional be called upon to render decisions requiring judgments about confidentiality, the duty to warn third parties, or other legal/ethical judgments, the fee clock can tick.

The preceding discussion should in no way prevent free or pro bono publico (for the people's good) work by counseling professionals. An important distinction should be made, however, between pro bono work and bad debts. The therapist must be able to choose who can therapeutically benefit from free services and for whom free services are only a continuation of noncompliant behavior. It is essential that both the counselor and client agree before services are rendered that the services will be free. Counselors should never reduce or waive fees after services have been rendered.

Collecting debts is both an art and a science. Although counseling professionals have the same legal rights as any other creditor, including the availability of small claims court for relatively small debts and higher courts for greater amounts, the decision to take a client to court is no small decision. The professional needs to consider that the payment recouped may not be worth the time and effort. Attorneys' fees, billable time lost, and the possibility that the professional will receive only a portion of the debt through garnishment of wages or liens militate against using the courts to redress nonpayment.

Another consideration is the possibility that the client-debtor may defend himself or herself with unkind gossip that may taint the professional. Many ethical complaints against counselors are filed with regulatory boards, national certification boards, and professional associations by clients who are retaliating after being sued for fee collection.

A further consideration is the legal duty to care for the patient, even if the patient is not amenable to care. The therapist who unilaterally neglects his or her clients or who leaves them without proper care, even for brief periods, may be sued for abandonment (Gutheil & Appelbaum, 1982), a breach of the duty to attend clients adequately. With respect to clients who repeatedly fail to pay their fees, the professional, again, must carefully document nonpayment, the pleas for compliance, the offer to see the client if the account is cleared, and referral to other (perhaps public) clinics. Essentially, the decision to take a client to court should be based upon dispassionate cost-benefit analysis, not upon getting even with a difficult client.

Another contract issue likely to become increasingly important for the mental health professional involves noncompetition clauses in employment contracts. Noncompetition clauses limit the type and location of the business in which the professional may engage after he or she leaves one employer and moves on to another. Generally, these covenants not-to-compete are designed to protect an employer from the competition a former employee can create. For example, a counseling agency may seek to restrict former employees from setting up a competing counseling practice in the same geographic area. Such an agreement has to be reasonable in its terms and not unduly restrict a counselor's right to make a living. Because *reasonable* means different things to different people (as well as courts), an attorney's help in determining fair and equitable terms is necessary.

A further contract issue becoming more prevalent is the inclusion of hold harmless clauses in mental health employment contracts (National Association of Social Workers, 1991). These clauses hold harmless the agency for which the counselor works in the event that both the agency and the counselor are sued. The counseling professional, even when covered by individual liability insurance, may be liable for agency attorneys' fees and damages against the agency. Some policies may not cover all these fees.

Given this trend, two options are available to mental health professionals. One is that they may contract for a rider on their liability insurance to cover the legal exposure in hold harmless clauses. Insurance providers, particularly those specializing in professional liability insurance, can increasingly be expected to offer such riders. Another option is that mental health professionals may try to negotiate away hold harmless clauses at the time of employment. Some employers may agree to eliminate such clauses from proposed employment contracts; however, others may not. In either case, it is up to the mental health professional to scrutinize his or her employment contract, to spot such clauses, and to negotiate, before signing. After signing a contract, the time for negotiating is past.

# Advertising

In mental health services as in every other industry, advertising is a tool for building professional image. It is a part of normal professional business expenses. Mental health agencies and counseling centers can use appropriate and tasteful advertising both to promote their services and to inform the public about mental health issues (Backover, 1991). Advertising is also part of counseling professionals' legal considerations.

Every state that licenses counseling professionals also places legal limits upon their advertising. Generally, limitations on the advertising of counseling services come in two varieties. In one, states tend to restrict the use of counseling titles. The restrictions with respect to advertising also apply to counseling agencies and businesses.

North Carolina law, for example, restricts the use of professional titles both for counseling professionals and for agencies:

> It shall be unlawful for any person who has not received a certificate of qualification as a Registered Practicing Counselor to assume or use such a title, or to use any words or other means of identification indicating that the person has been certified as a Registered Practicing Counselor, but such person may use the term *counselor* in connection with his [or her] name relating to his [or her] services as a counselor. (North Carolina 90-331, 1990)

In the other variety of limitation on advertising, states tend to restrict representations made to the public with respect to an individual's competency and experience to perform counseling. North Carolina law, for example, specifies the restricted use of advertising applied to mental health agencies and firms:

> It shall be unlawful for any firm, partnership, corporation, association, or other business or professional entity to assume or use the title of Registered Practicing Counselor, unless each of the members of such firm, partnership, or association first shall have received a certificate from the State Board of Registered Practicing Counselors. (North Carolina 90-332, 1990)

Violations of the North Carolina statutes (and similar statutes in other states) constitute misdemeanors. The sentences could include fines, imprisonment, or both.

States that regulate advertising by counseling professionals must balance two equally legitimate, but competing, public interests. The first interest is the state's interest in protecting public health and safety. If counseling professionals are allowed to make false or fraudulent claims, clients can be harmed and those who need to be helped may be inhibited from seeking help.

The second interest is in protecting commercial free speech. Commercial free speech allows a business or a person to advertise services to the public under First Amendment protection (*Central Hudson Gas v. Public Service Comm'n*, 1980). Essentially, state regulations on counseling advertising must find the least restrictive means possible to protect the public.

If state regulations overly restrict truthful advertising, they can be struck down by courts. In Nevada a family counseling center and its director sued to invalidate provisions of state regulations on advertising the costs and availability of counseling services. The Nevada Board of Marriage and Family Counselor Examiners code of ethics prohibited boldface type or other nonordinary typefaces as well as the listing of professional affiliations. The family counseling center advertised in boldface the specific counseling services it provided and the costs for a consultative session. The federal district court ruled that prohibitions against the truthful advertising of the availability and terms of counseling services may not be abridged (*Family Counseling Service of Clark Co. v. Rust*, 1978).

A New Jersey case illustrates how states have addressed issues relating to the advertising of counseling professionals. Plaintiff Sonnheim, who holds a master of social work degree and is a member of the Academy of Certified Social Workers (ACSW), was requested by the New Jersey State Board of Marriage Counselor Examiners to remove his name from the yellow pages listing under the category of Marriage and Family Counselors. Sonnheim refused. Subsequently, New Jersey Bell refused to accept Sonnheim's listing in this category without proof of his licensure as a marriage counselor. Sonnheim sued both the State Board of Marriage Counselor Examiners and New Jersey Bell to have his name in the yellow pages marriage classification and for monetary damages.

New Jersey law (45:8B-5, 1978) forbade anyone from advertising marriage counseling services, representing himself or herself as a marriage counselor, or using such a title as marriage counselor or family counselor unless he or she has been licensed by the State Board of Marriage Counselor Examiners. The Examiners argued that an advertisement under the marriage-counselor designation implies licensure and, consequently, when no licensure exists, misleads the public. Neither the trial court nor the court of appeals bought that argument.

The appeals court held that, by virtue of his professional degree and membership in ACSW, Sonnheim may represent himself as a marriage counselor without licensure by the State Board of Marriage Counselor Examiners (*Sonnheim v. State Board of Marriage Counselor Examiners*, 1982). The court also held that Sonnheim may advertise his services as a marriage counselor in the yellow pages. Thus, this appeals court struck the balance between protecting the public and free enterprise speech by allowing a graduate degreed person, certified by a national counseling association, to advertise as a marriage counselor without specific certification from a particular state agency.

Suggestions to ensure legally sound advertising for counseling professionals include the following:

1. **Check state regulations.** State law may regulate both the form and content of counseling services.
2. **Check ethical standards.** Examine appropriate and relevant ethical standards from both professional associations

and national certifying boards. Some ethical standards include rules applicable to advertising.
3. **Do not make quality claims that require verification.** Claims that treatments produce success rates and cures beyond those of other practitioners are hard to prove. They may also violate state criminal laws or state regulatory laws and open practitioners to civil suits.
4. **Make all information accurate and truthful.** Degrees and certifications should be clearly and accurately presented.
5. **All advertisements, whether print, radio, or television, should be reviewed and cleared by an attorney.** The advertiser will be held responsible for any defamatory remarks; for false, misleading, or fraudulent claims; or for advertisements that run counter to state mental health regulations. Approval from an attorney experienced in advertising law and/or mental health before the advertisement runs can ward off liabilities.

Copyright

American copyright law can trace its roots to 1556, when the English Stationer's Company was created by royal decree to help monopolize the printing business in order to stem the spread of the Protestant Reformation. The decree enabled the church and the government to control all printing and thereby censor works considered seditious or heretical (Latman, Gorman, & Ginsburg, 1985). Luckily, modern American copyright law has less insidious intentions. *Copyright* is the formal, legal name for protection against the theft of intellectual property.

Intellectual property includes articles, lectures, workshop curricula, and other creative works. Because the stock in trade of counselors, therapists, social workers, and other mental health professionals is intellectual in nature, the protection of intellectual property is as important to them as the protection of medical instruments is to a surgeon. The theft of intellectual property is as financially, personally, and professionally damaging to counseling professionals as the theft of equipment and data is to medical specialists.

Two laws currently direct American copyright enforcement. One is the Berne Convention that became effective in 1989 within the United States. This international convention's most salient feature is the abolishment of the notice of copyright for works published for the first time on or after March 1989 (Hammar, 1990). The other is the federal Copyright Act of 1976 that became effective in 1978. This Act protects "original works of authorship fixed in any tangible medium of expression, now known or later developed, from which they can be perceived, reproduced, or otherwise communicated, either directly or with the aid of a machine or device" (17 U.S.C. 90). This federal law expressly protects literary works; musical works; dramatic works; pictorial, graphic, and sculptural works; and motion pictures and sound recordings.

To qualify for copyright protection, a work must be able to claim both original authorship and tangible expression. For an author to claim copyright, he or she must have created it. Additionally, no copyright exists for mere thoughts or ideas not expressed in tangible form. If someone writes a book based upon an idea that you had 20 years before but did not express in any way, you have no legal recourse. Copyright protection gives the copyright holder exclusive rights to reproduce the work, to display it publicly, and to distribute copies either for sale or free.

A violation for illegally using another's copyrighted material is called an *infringement*. Federal copyright law provides civil and criminal penalties for copyright infringement (17 U.S.C. 501). Criminal infringements for financial gain or commercial advantage can carry penalties including forfeiture and destruction of the material. Additionally, fines not to exceed $2,500 can be assessed for fraudulently removing copyright notices, placing a fraudulent copyright notice on any article, or making false representations in applying for copyright registrations.

Courts have a number of civil options for infringement as well. These remedies include enjoining further infringement or impounding copies of the infringed material. An injunction is a legal restraint, in this case, of further infringement of the copyrighted object.

Perhaps the most potent civil penalty is liability for damages and profits gleaned from copyright infringement. Actual damages and profits may be awarded against the infringer. Instead of actual damages, the copyright owner may elect to collect statutory damages. Statutory damages, before final judgment, are set from $250 to $10,000 for the infringement of any one work. Where a court finds willful infringement, the costs can be set at $50,000 for each infringed work. Civil remedies can also include court costs and attorneys' fees.

This discussion of the costs of copyright infringement seeks to impress upon the reader the serious nature of stealing intellectual property. Publishers, editors, authors, and other copyright holders can be expected to pursue vigorously their copyright protections. Everyone who has made copies in any public place has seen copyright infringement signs on photocopy machines. Mental health professionals are vulnerable to infringement in their work as authors, teachers, consultants, and workshop leaders. Agencies and mental health centers can be sued equally along with private counselors.

Counseling professionals encounter copyright law in almost every aspect of their businesses. It is important to note that not actually taking money or making money from selling copyrighted material does not protect an infringer from civil and criminal penalties.

How can mental health professionals protect original, tangible works? The Copyright Act provides that, theoretically, original works are copyrighted as soon as they are made. Thus, from the moment that a mental health professional writes an article, it is copyrighted. The most common way to announce that your material is copyrighted is to place three elements on the article: (1) the copyright symbol (©), (2) the year the work was made, and (3) your name (thus: © Bullis, 1993). Placing this notice on original articles, charts, syllabi, diagrams, drawings, slide presentations, overhead projections, videotapes, and other work places others on notice that you intend to claim this as your own material. Despite the Berne Convention's abolition of the copyright notice, it is strongly recommended that publishers continue to place copyright notices on published works.

Registering your original work with the Copyright Office in Washington, DC, is a more formal way to protect your copyrighted material. Although registering your work is not a prerequisite for initial copyright protection, it is a legal requirement after publication. The registration requires a fee of $20.00 and two copies of the material. Write:

>Copyright Office
>Library of Congress
>Washington, DC 20559

A hotline number is also available for application forms at 202-287-9100. A variety of circulars are available on various copyright topics; those interested may request circular R2 from the Copyright Office.

In what ways may professionals violate copyright law? Mental health professionals may most commonly violate copyright law by not properly referencing others' copyrighted material included in their own work (plagiarism) and by illegally reproducing copyrighted material. Not giving credit where proper credit is due in lectures and speeches as well as in writing is an infringement. The Copyright Act provides limitations on infringement called *fair use* (17 U.S.C. 107). Fair use means that copyrighted material may be reproduced legitimately for criticism, fair comment, news reporting, scholarship, teaching, and research. The four factors determining fair use are (1) the purpose and character of the use, including whether the use is for commercial benefit or not-for-profit educational use, (2) the medium of the created work, (3) the amount and substantiality of the work used in proportion to the total work, and (4) the effect of the use on the potential market or value of the work.

Fair use is the statutory reason that scholars can quote each others' work (up to a point) without infringement if they properly cite the copyrighted material. However, it is a common misconception that merely referencing material gives license to duplicate it even if no money is earned for the presentation. (A duplicating business that makes multiple copies of excerpts from copyrighted books without permission and sells them to college students *is* guilty of infringement [*Basic Books, Inc. v. Kinko's Graphics Corp.*, 1991].) Note that duplicating entire articles or chapters for distribution at a lecture or a conference is an infringement. Such copying should never be done without the written permission of the holder of the copyright. Furthermore, duplicating testing booklets or scoresheets, and the logo or advertising copy of other mental health practitioners, is probably also an infringement.

Courts have not been lenient with copyright infringement, even where relatively small amounts of copied material are involved (Hammar, 1990). For example, one court held that copying eight sentences was infringement (*Martin Luther King, Jr., Center for Social Change, Inc. v. American Heritage Products, Inc.*, 1981). If in doubt, it is always judicious and professionally courteous to request permission to duplicate even small portions of another's work.

Who holds the copyright? The question warrants some discussion. When requesting permission to use copyrighted material, always check the copyright notification. Generally, it will be the publisher of the article or book. In some instances, it may be the author or another party. Thus, often the author does not hold the copyright and cannot give permission to duplicate his or her work.

Employment Discrimination

In 1964 President Johnson signed the Civil Rights Act into law and set into motion one of the most sweeping changes in employment in this century. The Act forbids employment discrimination based upon race, color, sex, national origin, or religion. It applies to all employers affecting interstate commerce who employ at least 15 workers. Although it is clear that this Act applies to employers of mental health professionals in colleges, universities, and state or federal mental health agencies, at first glance this legislation may seem not to apply to many private mental health agencies and centers. However, interstate commerce may include out-of-state consulting, teaching, speaking engagements, or other business activities. So even smaller agencies that do most of their business with in-state mental health activities may fall within the purview of federal employment laws. Additionally, they may fall within the purview of state employment laws.

The 1964 Civil Rights Act also established the Equal Employment Opportunity Commission (EEOC) to administer its employment rules. The Commission later received authority to enforce the Equal Pay Act as well as the Age Discrimination and Employment Act (ADEA). The Equal Pay Act, passed in 1963, was designed to end sex-based pay discrimination (Friedman & Strickler, 1987). Essentially, the Equal Pay Act requires that men and women be equally paid for work of "equal skill, effort, and responsibility." The ADEA, passed in 1967, outlaws discrimination with respect to age. The ADEA applies to private businesses engaged in commerce with at least 20 employees as well as state and local governmental agencies (Friedman & Strickler, 1987).

Generally, the EEOC has jurisdiction over employers with 15 or more employees, except for religious institutions for those employees working with religious activities. The EEOC has the power to ask for legal relief by reinstating or hiring employees, giving back pay, eliminating the discriminatory employment practice, and assigning the responsibility for the payment of reasonable attorneys' fees.

In 1991 President Bush signed into law the Civil Rights Reauthorization Act of 1991 (P. L. 102-167). This legislation affects mental health employers and employees in several ways (Ross, 1992). It reverses Supreme Court decisions (*Ward's Cove Packing Company v. Atonio*, 1989) that worked to shift the burden of proving discrimination to the putative victim. The burden of proof for proving employment discrimination now requires that the employer justify hiring and promotion practices that may appear to hinder women and minorities.

The burden of proof is significant, even crucial, in winning or losing discrimination cases. It is the standard by which the case is determined. The burden of proof determines who must do the proving and what that standard of proof is. For example, in criminal trials the burden is borne by the prosecutor and is the highest standard of proof beyond a reasonable doubt. This standard of proof might be described as convincing the jury that the defendant is guilty to 90% to 99% certainty. The next highest standard is clear and convincing evidence. This standard might be described as proving the evidence to 75% to 80%. The lowest standard of proof is preponderance of the evidence. This standard might be described as convincing to 51%. The 1991 Civil Rights Act, by shifting the burden of proof to the employer, influences the outcome of discrimination suits.

The Act also sets limits for the size of judgments against employers in discrimination cases. Limits are based on the number of employees. For example, agencies or counseling centers with between 15 and 100 employees have limits of $50,000 for discrimination suits. These limits apply to women, religious minorities, and disabled persons but do not apply to racial minorities.

It is clear that the 1991 Act presents both a challenge and a comfort for mental health employers with fewer than 100 employees. On one hand, employers might have the burden of convincing the courts that their allegedly discriminatory employment practices can be justified. On the other hand, except for racial discrimination, there is a cap on damages that employers must pay where discrimination is proved.

Sex Discrimination

Suits filed or brought under EEOC rules or sexual discrimination laws have included a case in which a New York City detective was awarded a promotion (Hays, 1991) and a case in which an accountant was awarded a partnership in one of the top American accounting firms (Lewin, 1991). These two cases serve to illustrate how sex discriminations arise and the possible penalties imposed.

In the first case, the detective filed a sex bias suit claiming that the New York City Police Department allowed an atmosphere of discrimination and harassment that caused her to lose promotions and pay. She filed the suit after she gave birth to her second child and returned to work in the Major Case Squad. The detective claimed her immediate supervisor assigned her to menial cases instead of her usual duties, which were investigating bank robberies and truck hijackings. She also claimed her immediate supervisor berated her for returning to work after having children, used disparaging remarks when referring to her, told a man assigned as her partner that he couldn't be much of a man if he consented to work with a "broad" detective, and refused to assign her cases likely to win citations and promotions. The detective and the department settled out-of-court.

The second case, *Hopkins v. Price Waterhouse*, 1989, has an important procedural history because it was one of the cases the Civil Rights Act of 1991 overturned. The Supreme Court held in *Hopkins* that the claimant has the initial burden of showing discrimination, and that the burden then shifts to the employer to prove innocence. Significantly, the Court also held that employers need only prove their case by a preponderance of the evidence, not by clear and convincing evidence. Of course, the new civil rights law now imposes a higher burden upon employers.

Ann Hopkins, the plaintiff in this case, was nominated for a partnership in her accounting firm—the only woman nominee among 88 candidates for promotion. She brought in more business than any other candidate, but she also received a greater number of negative comments from partners than any other candidate, mostly concerning her interpersonal skills. She sued, and the case was appealed up to the Supreme Court.

Upon retrial, Ms. Hopkins, who now works elsewhere, was awarded both a partnership in the firm and back pay amounting to $400,000. This result shows that courts will both hear discrimination suits based upon lost promotions and order reinstatement where deemed appropriate.

Pregnancy Discrimination

In 1978 Congress passed the Pregnancy Discrimination Act. This Act creates sanctions against employers with over 15 employees who take certain actions against pregnant employees (Slonaker & Wendt, 1991). These illegal actions include firing or essentially releasing an employee for becoming pregnant, refusing to hire a potential employee simply because she is pregnant, refusing to promote an employee simply because she is pregnant, demoting an employee or imposing other sanctions because of pregnancy, and denying fringe benefits, such as medical insurance, medical leave, and disability insurance, because of pregnancy.

Counseling offices and agencies need to avoid pregnancy discrimination just as much as other types of discriminations. Although it may be tempting to try to avoid the costs associated with pregnant employees by engaging in the proscribed behaviors, such tactics are illegal. Additionally, pregnancy discrimination is legally addressed in a similar manner as other protections under Title VII of the 1964 Civil Rights Act—and should be defended against in the same way.

Employers and supervisors need to know the options available to employees who feel discriminated against (Scott, 1990). First, employees can discuss their allegations explaining that they expect treatment equal to that of other employees. They may want to keep a log or diary of specific acts or words that will validate a claim of pregnancy discrimination.

Second, employees need to exhaust administrative remedies within the workplace. Employees may need to assert their claims before supervisors, unions, a personnel committee or department, or a human resource department. These decisions need to be appealed to the highest level of authority.

If these efforts fail and the employees want to continue prosecuting their claim, they need to check about filing a claim with the state human rights commission, state or federal EEOC, or other civil rights groups. It is important to remember that states may offer even greater protection than does federal legislation.

As in the case of sex discrimination and age discrimination, the employer should establish company policies that detail the nature of pregnancy discrimination, the company's opposition to such behavior, and administrative procedures for dealing with any complaints that arise. Legal advice always is recommended to ensure the legal rights of both employer and employee.

Affirmative Action

Title VII of the 1964 Civil Rights Act allows the court to order an affirmative action program if an employer has been judged to have engaged in intentionally discriminatory behavior. Such affirmative action programs may include the hiring or reinstatement of fired employees (Friedman & Strickler, 1987). Of course, employers may engage in voluntary affirmative action policies in order to correct an imbalance in the numbers of minorities on staff. Affirmative action laws, policies, and procedures are among the most contentious and complex and result in some of the most confusing decisions in all of employment law.

Policies and procedures driven by affirmative action principles have been both affirmed and stricken by courts. For example, when nonminority, tenured teaches were laid off during a school budget crisis while nontenured, minority teachers were retained, the nonminority teachers brought suit. The Supreme Court held that the action violated the Constitution (*Wygant v. Jackson Board of Education*, 1986). Such suits are often referred to as reverse discrimination suits—meaning that nonminority persons file a claim of discrimination.

Conversely, courts have allowed companies to proceed with affirmative action plans that give preferential treatment to minority persons. For example, a federal court could order a labor union, previously found to have engaged in discriminatory practices, to give employment preferences to minority persons who were not themselves victims of discrimination (*Local 28 of Sheet Metal Workers v. EEOC*, 1986).

Employers who promulgate affirmative action procedures need to draft them clearly and carefully. Therefore, legal and managerial advice from many quarters should be sought on the soundness of affirmative action policies. This is not an area for the legal or managerial generalist; specialists need to be consulted.

Disabilities

The Americans With Disabilities Act (ADA), enacted in 1990, requires that employers make "reasonable accommodations" in the workplace so as to cause no "undue hardship" for a broad range of employees with disabilities. Possible penalties for failure to abide by this law include the awarding of back pay, reinstatement, the levying of fines to cover attorneys' fees, and the paying of both compensatory and punitive damages. Federal regulations, specifically applying the ADA, have been issued (Code, 1991).

To help employers understand this important Act, Postol and Kadue (1991) offered a guide that includes such subjects as who is covered, who is not covered, and what reasonable accommodation is. Disabilities covered under this Act include epilepsy, heart diseases and conditions, former drug use, psychiatric problems, legal blindness (or blindness in one eye), leg amputation, arthritis, mental retardation, emotional illness, infection with the HIV virus, degenerative nerve and muscle diseases, and sensitivity to tobacco smoke.

There are also many conditions the ADA is not intended to cover. The Act expressly does not cover conditions of a sexual/legal nature including homosexuality, bisexuality, transvestitism, pedophilia, and voyeurism. The ADA does not cover the conditions of compulsive gambling, kleptomania, and current use of illegal substances. The ADA will apply to employers with over 15 employees in July 1994. From July 1991 until that time, the ADA will apply to employers with over 25 employees.

The ADA helps protect the covered classes of persons in several ways. It disallows sweeping inquiry, before a job is offered, as to whether a person is disabled or the nature and extent of such disability. The Act also disallows employment standards that unnecessarily exclude the protected classes from employment. This means that employers must distinguish between essential job requirements and those requirements that may be met by a reasonable accommodation on the employer's part.

Such accommodations are designed to enable the individual to perform essential job functions. They may include making facilities physically accessible to disabled employees; using adaptive hardware, including telephone headsets and special lighting equipment for visually impaired receptionists; using readers or interpreters for visually or hearing impaired employees; modifying examinations, training materials, or policies; using flexible work schedules; restructuring job requirements to eliminate nonessential job elements; or reassigning an employee to a vacant position (Postol & Kadue, 1991).

Finally, the ADA outlaws discrimination against employees because they live with or associate with the protected classes of handicapped persons. For example, the ADA prohibits discrimination against someone living with a person infected with the HIV virus or a person living with someone who is blind, deaf, or who has multiple sclerosis.

The Right of Privacy

Although other areas of the law affect labor-management relations, the right to privacy particularly deserves mention because the stock in trade of mental health employers is preserving the integrity of clients. However, the right of privacy is balanced against the legitimate needs of employers to determine the fitness of employees.

A separate tort has been created over the past several years for cases in which an employer (or others) unreasonably intrudes upon the privacy of another or publicly discloses private facts (Keeton, Dobbs, Keeton, & Owen, 1984). In the realm of employment law, courts have awarded damages to employees and potential employees whose privacy rights were violated. For example, highly personal and sensitive information such as forcing information about a wife's premarital relationships (*McSurely v. McClellan*, 1985) or repeated sexual questioning (*Phillips v. Smalley Maintenance Services*, 1983) may be regarded as unwarranted and illegal intrusions upon privacy rights. Other acts foreseeable in the context of mental health employment may also constitute an invasion of privacy. Sharing of an employee's medical records among other corporate employees may be impermissible if it is not done for legitimate business purposes (*Bratt v. IBM Corp.*, 1984).

The right to privacy is only a limited one, however. A doctor's note to a court describing a woman as an unfit mother was ruled not to be highly offensive and judged to have a legitimate public purpose (*Werner v. Kliewer*, 1985). Additionally, in an increasingly computerized, even mechanistic, society, the divulging of personal information easily accessible on computerized data bases does not violate privacy (*Peninsula Counseling Center v. Rahm*, 1986) nor does using polygraphs for reasonable and legitimate employment purposes, if not prohibited by state law (*Gibson v. Hummel*, 1985).

Sexual Harassment

The September 1991 confirmation hearings of Justice Clarence Thomas to the U.S. Supreme Court raised the nature and incidence of sexual harassment to new levels of national prominence. Since those hearings the issue of sexual harassment has become a serious political as well as employment issue. The basic test for employer liability in this area is whether the allegedly harassing conduct is pervasive, unwelcome, or sexually motivated, and if there is some legal basis for holding the employer liable (Goldberg, 1991).

The legal remedies for sexual harassment are not only available to individuals. A class action suit for sexual harassment was recently allowed for the first time (American Association of Sex Educators, Counselors, and Therapists, 1992). *Class action suit* means that an entire class of persons sues under the same claim. In this case 100 women brought suit claiming that their employer subjected them to a hostile work environment. Evidence included testimony of verbal abuse and touching by male co-workers as well as nude posters of women posted on the employer's premises.

Obviously, adult men and women do not suddenly become sexless creatures when they go to work each day, even in a counseling environment. A workplace free of sexuality is unrealistic and inhuman. Male and female co-workers can be expected to compliment each other on how they look, discuss sexual issues at work, and perhaps even to date. Supervisors in the helping professions can be expected to have a staff that will include sexuality as a part of its functioning. Employers and supervisors do have a legal obligation, however, to manage and monitor situations in which sexuality is a significant part of employee interrelations.

The EEOC defines *sexual harassment* as sexual advances or requests for sexual favors and other unwelcome verbal or physical sexual conduct when any one of the following conditions apply: (1) submission to such conduct is made explicitly or implicitly a condition of the alleged victim's employment, or (2) submission or rejection of such propositions is used as the basis for employment decisions affecting the victim, or (3) such propositions have the purpose or effect of unreasonably interfering with work performance of the victim or creating a hostile, intimidating, or offensive work environment (McGowan, 1991).

The U.S. Supreme Court later broadened employer liability by expanding the definition of sexual harassment: Employers are now liable not only if the harassment creates an offensive or hostile workplace but also if the harassment results in a firing or lost promotion (*Meritor Savings Bank v. Vinson*, 1986). Additionally, federal courts have ruled that nude pinups in the work place can constitute sexual harassment (*Robinson v. Jacksonville Shipyards, Inc.*, 1991) and that the standard for defining sexual harassment will no longer be the traditional "reasonable man" standard but what will offend "the reasonable woman" (*Ellison v. Brady*, 1991). However, courts continue to split on what specific behaviors constitute sexual harassment (Goldberg, 1991).

Sexual harassment is a charge that no employer wants and few can afford. This is particularly true for counseling agencies or mental health facilities. Monetary costs can arise from fines, civil judgments against offending companies, and employee absenteeism. For example, a 1991 law passed in Maine imposes fines of $5,000 to $10,000 for the first offense, $7,500 to $25,000 for the second offense, and $10,000 to $50,000 for the third offense ("Maine harassment law," 1991). Awards as high as $3.1 million have been awarded in state courts for successful sexual harassment suits. Furthermore, absenteeism, employee turnover, and low morale can cost a company up to $6.7 million each year (Clark, 1991).

The costs to a counseling or mental health agency sued for sexual harassment are even greater. Counseling agencies and mental health care institutions live and die by their reputation for treating clients with dignity, autonomy, and fair play. They do not sell just counseling services. They sell the image of client empowerment and self-respect. Counseling centers and agencies sued for sexual harassment risk the loss of both reputation and, therefore, clients. The risks for mental health employers, even to defend against an accusation of sexual harassment, are particularly great. Retaining lawyers and paying for court costs are expensive; and even if the suit fails or is unfounded, the agency must use its resources to announce its vindication in the media. Prevention is the most cost-effective approach to avoiding even the appearance of sexual harassment.

An Employer's Guide to Discouraging Unacceptable Behavior

How can employers help discourage sexual harassment in their workplace—and help avoid potential lawsuits? Supervisors need to be aware of the kind of sexual communications taking place among employees for three reasons. First, sexual harassment can undermine work productivity and be a source of friction among employees. Second, sexual harassment suits will be directed toward the employer. The employer is responsible for ensuring against sexual harassment in his or her workplace and will be held liable for failure to do so. Third, supervisors can set the tone for appropriate and inappropriate sexual communication between employees. A supervisor who can identify potential harassers and who can set clear standards for sexual conduct can go a long way toward preventing harassment, potential litigation, and the attendant publicity.

Potential types of harassing actions and the types of persons prone to such misconduct have been identified (Rosenfeld, 1991):

1. Jokes specifically designed to embarrass or humiliate others, or even those designed to make others blush, are inappropriate. Jokes or sexual communications designed to arouse another, without his or her consent, are also sexually harassing.
2. Dinner date requests, where not clearly a part of the work day, without a prior friendship, or mutual interest in developing a relationship, are out of line.

3. Touching a co-worker is not usually a good idea. Patting or touching the arm or shoulder in appropriate situations as a gesture of good will or sympathy is probably acceptable. Fanny patting, pinching anywhere, shoulder massages, or caressing with hands, eyes, or any other part of the anatomy is rude, unprofessional, and probably actionable.
4. Those who scoff at taking sexual harassment laws and charges seriously like to complain "You can't even compliment any more!" That is simply not true. Compliments on clothing, hairstyles, and other aspects of looks, demeanor, or work activity are a normal part of working relationships. Compliments that specifically refer to sexual anatomy or sexual acts, remarks that are designed to intimidate or offend, and suggestions that are intended as "come ons," however, may constitute harassment.
5. Flirting is a cloud in the already gray area of sexual harassment. The friendliness and lighthearted playing associated with flirting may not constitute a hostile working environment. Oppressive, crude, and offensive behavior constitutes hostility. However, those who flirt cannot expect their romantic expectations to be met and must maturely deal with unfulfilled expectations. In other words, although flirting does not constitute sexual harassment, potential resentments and frustrations must be addressed outside the workplace.
6. A short skirt or tight pants in the workplace or anywhere else is not an invitation to seduction. Such clothing does not mean that harrassing jokes or behavior will or should be tolerated. Clothing, particularly in the workplace, is not a moral barometer but an expression of style. A supervisor's wearing tight pants or seductive dresses does not constitute permission to make inappropriate advances or to make lurid jokes. By the same token, an employee who also wears provocative clothing is not giving permission for sexual harassment. Clothing style does not give license for inappropriate behavior.

Employers have three important tools for preventing sexual abuse in counseling offices. The first is the supervisor's own example. The second is a written policy against sexual harassment. The third is continuous education.

The supervisor's own example can discourage a climate in which sexual harassment creates a hostile work environment.

Where inappropriate jokes, touching, teasing, and flirting are not tolerated by supervisors, supervisors set an example of professionalism and respect for employees and colleagues.

A written policy against sexual harassment places employees on notice that behaviors creating a hostile work environment will not be tolerated. Such a policy should be clear, specific, and enforced. The policy should specify the behaviors that are prohibited, the method of complaints, and the procedures by which complaints will be addressed. The policy should specify the administrative sanctions imposed. Most importantly, the policy should be enforced strictly so that employees know that the policy and procedures both will protect them and will be used against them.

Continuous education should be directed toward the nature, causes, and consequences of sexual harassment. As new issues, statutes, law cases, and policies against harassment emerge, employees should be plainly and consistently informed. This new information can be disseminated in any number of ways, including newsletters, in-service training sessions, employee newsletters, and professional journals. The most effective tool is face-to-face education and training, with the opportunity for concerns and questions to be freely aired.

An Employee's Guide to Addressing Sexual Harassment

How can employees protect themselves from actual or potential sexual harassment? What legal steps can they take to file formal charges of sexual harassment?

Counseling professionals are often employees. They—and their employers—need to know their rights and obligations in order to best understand their own legal positions.

Employees need to know the rules. Sometimes just knowing the rules of sexual harassment is sufficient to intimidate a harasser. In any case, knowing the rules can dispel timidity or uncertainty about pressing a claim of harassment or confronting a harasser.

Employees need to keep score. If the Anita Hill-Clarence Thomas experience demonstrates anything, it is the importance of keeping careful records of allegedly harassing behavior. This record should include behaviors, possible witnesses, dates, and places where the alleged harassment took place. Essentially, a victim needs evidence, and plenty of it, to pursue a complaint successfully—either through the employer or the EEOC. Additionally, if a harasser knows someone is taking notes, he or she may stop.

Employees need to talk back. Clearly and consistently saying that someone's sexual comments are unwanted, unwelcome, offensive, or upsetting can serve three purposes. First, saying "no" places the offender on notice that such comments or other behaviors are indeed bothersome and that the victim has no intention of pursuing a sexual encounter of any kind. In less severe cases, such a negative response is enough to discourage further harassment. Second, saying "no" strengthens the victim's case. If the victim documents evidence that he or she has repeatedly said "no," it is easier to persuade a court or grievance board that the victim has repeatedly warned the harasser. Try using the exact language of sexual harassment law to intimidate harassers enough to make them stop. Say "I think that comment qualifies as creating an offensive work environment, and I'll bet the company grievance board (or EEOC) thinks so too. Are you a gambler?" Although some may consider this remark to be pompous or pretentious, a victim who can voice it is more likely to be taken seriously than one who offers a meek or self-conscious protest. Those who threaten to file a complaint, of course, should be prepared to do so.

Employees can file a formal complaint. Filing a complaint is listed last precisely because filing a civil or administrative complaint is no small task. Generally, it is less traumatic and emotionally draining to settle harassment complaints on a personal level. In general, filing should be used only as a last resort.

Employer Vicarious Liability

Employers of counseling professionals can be held liable for the negligent acts of their employees. This general class of negligence actions is sometimes called *vicarious liability*. Employer vicarious liability is a relatively new, but fertile, area of liability for counseling negligence. Although theories of vicarious liability are relatively recent, they constitute the basis for a significant amount of the litigation against counselors and their agencies and employers.

Theories of vicarious liability are used with frequency by plaintiffs primarily for two reasons. The first is that the trend of recent years seems to be increasingly flexible in allowing plaintiffs to sue employers. Many states allow two or more theories of liability to hold employers vicariously liable for the wrongdoings of their employees. The second reason is that agencies and mental health employers have deeper pockets than most individual mental health professionals. Without the ability to collect on an award, a court victory is a hollow win.

Employer vicarious liability negligence actions are generally based on *respondeat superior* and its three legal children: negligent hiring and retention, negligent supervision, and negligent training. It is important for supervisors and employers to know and understand these four theories because their agencies and counseling centers are vulnerable to suits. Additionally, supervisors and employers can take defensive steps to avoid such suits if they know the plays of the offense. Although these theories may seem similar, almost redundant, the law sometimes turns upon the sharp edge of precise words. All the theories are important because when one theory fails, liability may be imposed under another.

1. Respondeat Superior

Respondeat superior, the label most commonly applied to a legal action against employers for the negligence of employees, is a Latin phrase meaning "Let the master answer." Under respondeat superior, an employer's liability for the acts of employees revolves around the amount of control an employer can exert over an employee. A number of different tests are used to determine the degree of control. For example, when a clergy therapist engaged in sexual relations with a client, respondeat superior liability was imposed upon the counseling center even though the acts were clearly not the acts the therapist was paid to perform (*Doe v. Samaritan Counseling Center*, 1990). The court held that negligent acts that arise out of and are "reasonably" incident to legitimate job requirements satisfy the control element for vicarious liability.

Perhaps even more significant than this rather broad interpretation of respondeat superior is the fact that liability was imposed even though the sexual acts occurred during the month after the client canceled therapy. The court reasoned that liability should still be imposed because the counseling relationship was seen as initiatory to the sexual relationship. The court also reasoned that the misuse of the transference phenomenon (obviously begun during counseling) was so connected with the counseling process that there was a very close connection with the negligent acts and the counseling. Clearly, even when negligent acts do not occur during the time limits of the therapeutic relationship, vicarious liability may still be imposed.

Certainly not all courts will rule this way. Other courts might have taken a more restrictive view of the control element. However, there is a growing public awareness and expressed disapproval of professional misconduct, particularly sexual misconduct. Indeed, some states have passed statutes criminalizing sexual activity with current and, under certain circumstances, past clients. Thus, the policy of courts may be increasingly to allow for employer liability for intentional misconduct by mental health professionals.

Avoidance of such cases obviously involves screening prospective mental health practitioners, continuing education, and strong employer leadership and supervision. A hard fact for mental health employers is that the concept of respondeat superior has expanded in recent years. Today, even if a claim under respondeat superior fails, the similar theories of negligent hiring and retention, negligent supervision, and negligent training may prevail to hold the employer liable.

2. Negligent Hiring and Retention

The theory of negligent hiring and retention after hiring takes place, like respondeat superior, heavily depends upon a finding of a foreseeable risk by the employee and a neglect of that risk on the part of the employer for the lawsuit to succeed. A *foreseeable risk* means that a reasonable employer knew or should have known that an employee posed a danger to the public.

The increased availability of negligent hiring suits poses an increased duty on employers to investigate potential or current employees (Silver, 1987). Such investigations require checking applicants' references and further checking applicant backgrounds if there are suggestions of unethical or illegal behavior. If an employer discovers that a current or potential employee's counseling license has been suspended (even though it has been reinstated), the employer should ascertain the truth of this information, determine the nature of the offense, and find out the current licensure status of the employee as well as any remediation that has taken place.

3. Negligent Supervision

Negligent supervision is another form of respondeat superior. As in respondeat superior, the crucial question is whether the wrongful action was within the *scope of employment*. The action seems to be more often labeled as such when the employee has greater discretion in his or her job function. This is most likely the case for most mental health practitioners.

Courts seem to be split as to whether to take more or less strict reading of scope of employment. For example, two courts sitting in two different states made contrary rulings in cases in which therapists engaged in sexual relations with clients and were sued under the theory of negligent supervision. In one case, the U.S. Court of Appeals, sitting in Washington State and operating under its laws, ruled that a counselor engaged in a sexual relationship with a client acted within the scope of his employment with the Indian Health Service (*Simmons v. United States*, 1986). The client sued the counselor's employer, in this case the federal government, for injuries under a theory of negligent supervision. The test the court used in making its determination was a broad one: whether the counselor was engaged at the time in furtherance of the employer's interests.

The court then reasoned that though the counselor was not authorized to engage in sexual activities with a client, he did make the sexual contact while engaged in his legitimate counseling activities. That is, if the counselor had not been in a position of counseling the woman, the relationship would not have developed. This furtherance test is a broad one and can subject the employer to an array of suits under negligent supervision. The court found that the employer could be held liable for the counselor's alleged misconduct.

One year later a New Jersey court came to an opposite conclusion when faced with the same issue tried under the same theory of negligent supervision. The therapist engaged in sexual activities with a client over a period of a year. The client and her husband sued the therapist and his two employers, in this case state and county departments (*Cosgrove v. Lawrence*, 1987). The court ruled that sexual relationships were not the kind of conduct for which the therapist was hired and not within the scope of employment. Thus, no liability attached to the employer.

4. Negligent Training

The final, and perhaps newest, theory of employer vicarious liability is negligent training. Because the mental health field is constantly adding new knowledge and skills to its professional repertoire, this form of liability can be expected to attach to counseling and counseling education soon and with some frequency. The elements of this negligence action are similar to, and often complement, a primary claim of negligent hiring and retention (Fenton, Ruud, & Kimbell, 1991). The crux of a claim for negligent training is a foreseeable risk to third parties where responsible training could have averted the risk.

For example, a woman who was raped in her parking deck collected damages for negligent training against the employers of security guards hired to protect such customers (*Erikson v. Curtis Investment Co.*, 1988). The *Erikson* court held that the security company should reasonably have foreseen that such an assault was possible and that proper training could have averted such an assault.

When this criterion is applied to mental health professionals, an employer could be expected to provide adequate training for, say, suicide prevention, prevention of dual relationships with clients, and prevention of professional fraud and misrepresentation. Such training could take any number of forms, including in-service training and training by an outside consultant.

The following guidelines (adapted from Fenton, Ruud, & Kimbell [1991] to mental health professionals) should help avoid this form of vicarious liability:

1. Prior to employment, make sure candidates have all the required licensure and academic degrees necessary for the job. If the position requires state licensure and other credentials, make sure that the employment file contains copies of such licensure, graduate transcripts, and other necessary documents *certified from their original source* prior to employment.
2. Employers should require employees to attend professional education seminars. Such seminars should be reasonably related to the clients or populations addressed by the employee. Evidence of such attendance should be part of the employee's file.
3. Employees should be trained in the policies and procedures of the agency or counseling center in which they work. This training should emphasize the behaviors that the employer will not tolerate, how the policies and procedures are enforced, and how employee acts should be designed to protect any third-party (including the employee's) interest, health, and safety.
4. Employers should develop and implement a training and education program for mental health employees. These programs should be designed to address gaps between current skills and the skills necessary to fulfill the most stringent

demands of clients and student supervisees or the issues they present. Such training programs should be based on individual employee needs and the likely needs of the clients or profession. Clear, attainable training objectives need to be established, and after the training is completed, follow-up evaluations need to be conducted to ensure that the training has indeed met those objectives.

Adapted by permission from the June 1991 Issue of the *Labor Law Journal*, published and copyrighted 1991 by Commerce Clearing House, Inc., 4025 W. Peterson Avenue, Chicago, Illinois 60646. All Rights Reserved.

Agency

Agency is a small word for a big idea. *Agency* can be defined as a fiduciary relationship that is established when two people agree that one will act on behalf of another. The agent works on behalf of another—his or her master or principal. This fiduciary relationship means that agents have a special, legal responsibility to their *principals*—those for whom they are agents.

Mental health professionals need to know the general law of agency for two reasons. As employees, they need to know when they, wittingly or unwittingly, act as agents for their employers. Acting as an agent carries with it legal rights and obligations. As employers and supervisors, they need to know when they, wittingly or unwittingly, empower their employees with the legal capacity of agents.

Reuschlein and Gregory (1990) discussed both (1) the duties of agents and (2) the ways in which the legal duties of agents are created:

1. Acting as an agent means that the agent must act in special and specific ways relative to the principal and has fiduciary, loyalty, and obedience duties. The essential element of fiduciary duty is that the agent be trustworthy in all dealings concerning the principal. The agent should, at all times, deal honestly and forthrightly with the principal.

   The duty of loyalty requires that the agent always act in the best interests of the principal. This means that the agent must always subordinate his or her personal goals, agenda, or interests to those of the principal. The agent must always faithfully respond to the principal's wishes and requirements.

The duty of obedience requires that the agent always obey the instructions, limitations, and contractual agreements of the principal. This duty means that the agent must truthfully report all transactions and dealings to the principal. In turn the agent must honestly convey the principal's intentions to others.

2. Real and incidental authority emerge as primary ways by which agency can be granted. *Real authority* means that the principal has been informed and specifically consents to the agent's acting on his or her behalf. The clearest way to establish real authority in the agent is for the principal to write down exactly what the agent can and cannot do. Sometimes, the law will also recognize oral instructions from the principal as creating real authority in the agent.

A problem that arises from express, detailed instructions from a principal is that all contingencies that must be addressed are not covered in written agreements. The principal cannot always foresee every contingency. So the law allows the agent some latitude to carry out his or her real authority. This is *incidental authority* and conveys powers to the agent not expressly delegated by the principal. For example, real authority to manage a mental health center would also include the incidental authority to hire and fire counseling professionals.

A primary way that agency law applies to the counseling business is in partnerships. When two or more counseling professionals form a commercial partnership, they may also be allowing each of the partners to act as an agent on behalf of the partnership. Simultaneously, each partner is then a principal in relation to the agent. For example, if Joan and Joe form a partnership and consent to have each other act on behalf of the partnership, both Joan and Joe are agents (when they act on behalf of the other) and principals (when they are the ones who consent to the other's acting as an agent).

This commercial relationship may get complicated if Joe and Joan do not agree on the limits to their capacities as agents. What if Joe buys a new copier and fax machine for the partnership? Joan could be responsible for Joe's purchases on behalf of the partnership, if he is given broad authority. Another example is where one partner signs contracts for office space, office machines, or maintenance. Without clear, written authorizations about who can act as agent for the partnership, what the spending limits are, and what kind of contracts may be signed, the other partners may be liable for the unauthorized spending of one of their partners.

In addition, people who think they have the power and authority to act as agents may be in for a rude shock when they discover that they are personally responsible for the contract that they have signed. For example, a department head of a public mental health agency may allow a new employee to get some furniture for his or her office. Should the employee spend too much money on a new desk, computer, and end tables, some department heads might refuse to pay. Of course, it may be that the sellers never should have taken an order from an employee without verification from a supervisor. Certainly, the question of legal authority to make such purchases will arise. In the end, the employee may be personally responsible for the purchases. Either way, clear directions on the limitations and allowances for agency actions by the employee could have prevented such costly inconvenience.

Furthermore, what if an agent gains business information that the agent uses to compete against his or her principal? This could happen if an agent, himself or herself a counseling professional, discovers that lucrative employee assistance contracts will be negotiated. If the agent uses his or her information to bid against the principal, the agent may violate his or her fiduciary duties. Such violations could cause the agent to be liable to the principal for economic losses.

Insurance

Adequately protecting your mental health practice is no longer a luxury. Such protection should be considered a normal and routine business expense. Counseling professionals need not only insurance against theft, fire, slip-and-fall cases, and malpractice but also, for example, insurance against employment discrimination, sexual harassment, copyright infringement, and breach of fiduciary responsibilities. The American Counseling Association's Member Insurance Programs offer an audiocassette (free to members) that discusses liability insurance issues.

Getting the proper insurance, given the current litigious climate, is, however, more complicated than paying the premiums on time. Several considerations are important in deciding from whom to buy the insurance and in choosing which coverage to seek.

Whom should you buy the insurance from? Security and solvency are of primary importance. Essential considerations in selecting an insurance carrier, according to the director of ACA Insurance Programs (Nelson, 1991), include the following:

1. Is the insurance company financially sound? Many sources can help determine the financial health of insurance carriers. A.M. Best publishes a rating of insurance companies. Many states, which regulate the insurance industry, will release data on insurance companies licensed to operate in their states. The state insurance regulatory body may be willing to disclose, for example, the types and numbers of complaints about a given insurance company. Discussing insurance plans

with friends and colleagues may also be a helpful way to gain information.
2. Have the insurance premiums (rates) been fairly steady over time? Stability is a sign of security in the insurance industry. When rates take unexpected, unprecedented upturns, it may be a sign of financial or managerial difficulties. Although insurance costs can be expected to take normal cost-of-living hikes, rate fluctuations over a period of time can mean a softening financial base or impending corporate trouble.
3. What is the insurance company's claim payment record? Some insurance companies pay claims expeditiously. Others do not. The issue here is not the nonpayment of false or inappropriate claims, but the slow or overly-complicated payment of claims clearly covered by the policy. Again, insurance raters such as A.M. Best as well as state insurance regulators may provide data on the timeliness of claim payments.

What coverage should you seek? Specific issues and suggestions in determining insurance needs and selecting an insurance policy include the following:

1. Read the policy carefully for its terms of coverage. Several factors need to be considered in determining the types of coverage. Beyond the usual business coverage for property damage, theft, personal injury, and malpractice, specific terms need to be examined:

   - Determine if the malpractice coverage is retroactive.
   - Determine if legal defense costs, even for frivolous claims, will be paid by the insurance company. Defending even a meritless claim for, say, malpractice can be expensive when legal fees, court costs, and lost work time are cumulated. Look for insurance that covers the defense costs for all claims against you or your agency or organization.
   - Determine if the coverage includes both intentional and unintentional claims. The counseling professional needs to know whether criminal acts, malicious acts of commission or omission, or other exclusions apply. Limitations of coverage against certain claims are also important. The counseling professional should know the extent of coverage for each allegation or type of allegation.

Of course, your ability to afford the premiums is an important consideration. Most professionals will purchase using a cost-benefit analysis. How much insurance can a given practitioner afford to buy without becoming "insurance poor"? This question is best answered by the individual mental health professional given his or her financial status. A strict scrutiny of the terms of the policy and the realistic needs of the practitioner, however, can determine the necessary coverage for the best possible costs.

2. Consider personal insurance even if you work for an agency or department with its own insurance. As already noted, mental health professionals who work for agencies or departments that provide insurance for them still need to consider individual insurance plans. The liability of individual professionals may differ from the liability for corporate entities such as state agencies, partnerships, or privately owned corporations. Therefore, the legal vulnerabilities are also different.

Many malpractice suits name both the mental health professional and the agency as defendants (see the section on Employer Vicarious Liability). For example, the agency may wish to make an out-of-court settlement with the plaintiff, admitting some guilt on the clinician's part and some on the agency's part thus avoiding a costly court battle and even greater money damages. This may be attractive for some parties, but for the clinician it could be both personally and professionally devastating.

To address these more complex business insurance needs, some companies offer two alternatives (P. L. Nelson, personal communication, December 31, 1991). First, some policies offer business owner's policies (BOP) for small businesses. Second, insurance for the incorporated business can often be added to policies just designed to cover individual mental health professionals.

Another relatively new development in mental health professional insurance brings this issue into even greater focus. Some employers now want counseling professionals to sign hold harmless agreements as a condition of employment (National Association of Social Workers, 1991). Hold harmless clauses work to exempt the employing agency or department from any liability associated with the employee's work. Although this publication addresses this issue in the section on

Contracts, the insurance implications beg discussion. Under hold harmless provisions, the individual mental health professional will be liable for damages such as court costs, attorneys' fees, and other costs if the suit succeeds. Yet, the professional will not be covered by the agency insurance plan for such costs. Without private, independent insurance, the practitioner must pay with his or her own funds.

3. Consider additional features of insurance plans. Insurance plans can also cover lost earnings for lost time due to court appearances, depositions, and other suit-related lost earnings. During a protracted suit, or even a relatively minor suit, insurance against such lost earnings can mean the difference between an annoyance suit and a financially devastating suit.

Legal Audits

In order to prevent lawsuits and client complaints, major corporations employ large legal staffs to keep abreast of changing business laws and regulations as well as of changing client expectations. Individual mental health practitioners and even the larger agencies of mental health professionals cannot hope to pay for such extensive legal advice. Mental health practitioners and agencies can, however, conduct legal audits. This section addresses why and how to conduct such legal audits.

Initiating and maintaining business practices and procedures to prevent lawsuits and client complaints by keeping up with new developments is as important for the mental health agency, department, and business as it is for any other kind of agency, department, and business. Laws change. For example, the law for mental health professionals can change radically and materially, as it did in 1976 when the court's decision in *Tarasoff v. Regents, University of California* (1976) initiated the duty of therapists to warn third parties when a client threatens harm. Some state statutes now impose this duty. The law surrounding the business of providing mental health services can change just as radically and materially, as it did with the passage of the Copyright Act of 1978 and the various employment discrimination laws, including the Americans With Disabilities Act of 1990.

Client expectations also change. Some of these expectations are reasonable; others are not. However, clients with unreasonable expectations can file lawsuits. The days of the untouchable professional are long gone. Clients are more consumer conscious about professional mental health services and increasingly demand accountability and efficiency. Insurance companies that reimburse clients for counseling services also expect a high degree of accountability and efficiency and do not hesitate to audit practitioners and to bring both civil and criminal charges where warranted.

A two-pronged legal audit can be undertaken regularly by mental health professionals to keep up to date and meet the needs of their practices and businesses. The first prong is to identify potential issues indicating liability. The second is to identify potentially litigious clients.

1. Identify Potential Liability Issues

Many of the major issues giving rise to liability have been identified in preceding sections, although no one publication can hope to cover all the possible issues. An important generalization can be made, however: The management of records and the expectations of clients (whether realistic or not) are two variables that surface again and again as bases for litigation. As one lawyer put it bluntly, "An attorney's thin file becomes a fat target in an action for legal malpractice" (Grasso, 1989). The same holds true for mental health professionals.

Maintaining thick files on even short-term clients is therefore essential. These files should include intake evaluations, copies of signed consent forms, treatment plans, diagnostic tests, session notes, and other pertinent data. Session notes are particularly important. They should include suggestions and directives made by the professional to the client and the responses of the client. Keep in mind that these are notes that may be brought into court records through the legal process of discovery. These notes can provide evidence that the professional offered the client a variety of tests, referrals, or other resources. Such suggestions, and more specifically the evidence of such suggestions, may mean the difference between a solid or weak defense against a client complaint. *Documentation in Counseling Records*, another publication in The ACA Legal Series, discusses similar matters at length.

Supervisors should see that these files are properly and regularly updated as well as securely maintained. The best plans and procedures for properly maintained files are useless if the system is not maintained in practice. In defending against vicarious liability, mental health employers have a vested interest in ascertaining that files are kept current. Supervisors can periodically and randomly check files and expect employees to keep files accurate and updated. Employers can also instill in professionals that documenting client and professional behavior is not mere paperwork, but rather liability control. Files not in active use should be kept in locked file drawers; permanent and particularly important files should be secured in fire-proof file cabinets.

Keeping personnel files complete and current is essential. Employers should maintain active files of credentials, employee training plans (as indicated in the discussion of respondeat superior), continuing education or other professional classes and seminars, academic and licensure credentials, performance evaluations, and other pertinent data.

Professional journals and business newspapers like the *Wall Street Journal* can be excellent sources of business law and regulation, as can in-service training seminars, particularly in mental health business information on law and regulation. At the very least reading and participating in training can provide enough information to suggest that either the law or business prudence requires additional help from an attorney or employment specialist.

Regularly reviewing policies and procedures with an attorney well versed in employment and business law—especially mental health business law if possible—is also essential. Larger government agencies and departments as well as larger private counseling and development corporations may have access to legal counsel. Most smaller agencies and private mental health centers can afford limited counsel with an attorney—especially when the centers use books such as this to formulate and to focus their questions and concerns. Additionally, some law firms offer seminars and other relatively inexpensive means to provide counseling and development firms with legal counsel.

Some clinicians have the erroneous notion that keeping no records, or very few records, will prevent proving a lawsuit against them. Their reasoning may be that "what they can't read, they can't prove." Such reasoning is erroneous for two reasons. First, the mental health professional can always be subpoenaed to testify at court or in a deposition. Either way, the testimony is under oath, and any misrepresentation or falsehood can be criminally prosecuted as contempt of court. Second, a lack of information on the professional's part is unlikely to be favorably treated by either a judge or a jury. After all, it is the professional, not the client, who is accountable for his or her actions and must have the documentation to substantiate treatment.

2. Identify Potentially Litigious Clients

Identifying those types of clients most likely to bring complaints or suits is the second prong of a legal audit. Although such clients cannot be identified with specificity or certainty, some types of clients seem to be more prone to bring suit, and the mental health professional can adopt preventive measures in such cases. These client types include the angry client, the disobedient client, the dishonest client, the bossy client, and the client who "just does not understand" (Robbins, 1991). Although these types originally applied to the clients of lawyers and are not described in clinical terms, mental health practitioners can translate such personalities into their own terms.

Angry clients want revenge and blame everyone else for their bad luck, failed relationships, and troubles. It may be only a matter of time before the anger gets directed toward the mental health professional. Unfortunately, suits can serve as a way of getting back at counselors, educators, and mental health employers and others in the "system" or in authority. The disobedient client will not accept recommendations and instructions—and may actually commit illegal or unethical acts. These clients may go way beyond resistance to certain exercises and treatment modes and expose the professional to claims of complicity in such acts as child abduction, spouse abuse, or fraud against the express direction of the professional.

Closely associated with the disobedient client is the outright dishonest client. The dishonest client materially misrepresents his or her life to the professional and to others. At an extreme, this client may try to implicate, or initiate conspiracies with, the professional in tax fraud, fraud against an insurance carrier, or misrepresentation of facts to a court on such issues as child custody, divorce, or other personal matters. Finally, and perhaps most dangerous, is the client who simply will not understand the direction and instruction of the mental health professional. Such misunderstanding can be most legally damaging when this type of client returns consent forms unsigned, does not comply with office forms and procedures, or experiments with therapeutic techniques against the advice of the professional.

Each of these types of clients poses legal and ethical challenges to the mental health professional that may land the agency or business in court or before a disciplinary review board. Acting proactively with these types of clients is the surest way to guard against potential legal vulnerabilities. Terminating a client may be the best option in some of these cases. When terminating a client, the cite-and-write rule should be followed. This rule directs that all specific instances of behavior that place the professional in ethical or legal jeopardy should be documented and filed—as should notations of the responses of the professional and client. Referral suggestions as well as correspondence related to the termination should also be noted. In this way, the mental health professional creates a record of the evidence for his or her actions.

Less drastic measures with the suit-prone client types might include using waivers and disclaimers. Waivers and disclaimers are signed documents, placed in the client's file, indicating that the client has been appraised of pertinent information that he or she chooses either to ignore or otherwise disregard. For example, if a client refuses to seek the advice of another professional for further medical or diagnostic testing, if a client refuses to sign a consent form to allow access to previous counseling records or to discuss the case with other professionals, or if the client refuses referrals, a letter signed by the client in the file should document both what options were offered and the client's refusal.

Such considerations on identifying litigious types are true also for prospective employees. Past references, academic credentials, professional accreditations, employment records, recommendations, and other preemployment documents should all be intact prior to the person's beginning work. Any delay or unwillingness to comply with requests for appropriate information should be treated with caution if not suspicion. As indicated in the discussions of employer vicarious liability, a complete and updated employee file is no longer a luxury. It is an absolute necessity.

Finally, an attorney versed in the mental health industry should be retained to help the agency or business conduct an annual review of its employment and business policies and procedures. At the very least this legal counsel should be consulted in times when substantial changes in business practices are imminent. A retained attorney can offer legal counsel when the business faces an urgent professional issue requiring a prompt response.

Frequently Asked Questions

Q. Why do I need additional insurance to cover my private practice (or public agency) when all my staff are individually covered by their own professional insurance plans?

A. It may be advisable to get additional coverage for your business because you may be sued individually as well as corporately. The individual insurance covers your personal losses, but you may need protection also to cover the losses (or potential losses) to your business. Suing the institution as well as the individual is becoming increasingly attractive as plaintiffs sense that businesses generally have more money than individual counseling professionals and as some states make it more legally possible to sue organizations for allegations.

Q. If I work for an agency or other institution that covers me under their general insurance policy, do I still need individual coverage?

A. Exploring this option is a good idea for at least three reasons. First, the corporate policy protects the business interests, not necessarily the individual mental health professional. This not-so-subtle difference could mean that if the insurance company determines that the suit is not worth litigation (going to trial), the insurance company may decide to settle the claim. This may leave the impression that the professional was, to some degree, guilty of the allegations lodged against him or her. Without the professional's own insurance to pay for an individual defense, the professional may have no other fiscal choice but to go along with the settlement, even though it may cause harm to him or her professionally.

Second, some corporate insurance policies have hold harmless clauses. These clauses allow the mental health professional to be liable for attorneys' fees and other costs assessed if a suit succeeds against both an agency and the professional. Additional, individual insurance can protect the professional working under this clause.

Third, the agency may conclude that its own legal interests diverge from that of the counselor-employee. For example, the agency may decide that it is in its best interests to settle the case or to make other legal decisions that may contradict the best interests of the individual counselor.

Q. I hardly ever make a written contract with my clients. We usually agree to the terms of mental health help verbally. Is this wrong?

A. Not in all cases. But the reasons for making a written contract with all clients are compelling. Simply the process of negotiating terms can be helpful, and negotiating terms can help both the professional and the client formulate their own reasonable expectations and hopes for results. A written document is hard to argue with if there is some misunderstanding. A written document is also a firm starting point for discussions should one or both sides want to change the contract. In addition, a written document protects the professional in the event a client accuses the professional of not abiding by the fee schedule, the time, place, and length of appointments, and other particulars.

Q. I work for a small firm that neither employs 15 or more people nor conducts interstate business; some of the federal employment laws apply only to those who do. Why do I still need to know about these laws?

A. It is important to know about employment discrimination laws for two reasons. One is that it is important to determine whether your office or business is covered either by state or federal employment discrimination laws. To make such a determination, legal counsel or knowledge of the laws is crucial.

The other reason is more philosophical. Even if your agency is not covered by the discrimination laws, counseling and human development professionals may find it helpful to examine such laws to formulate policies regarding, for example, pregnancy leave, sexual harassment, disabled persons, or affirmative action. It may be the case that counseling and development professionals may find it professionally advantageous and ethically responsible to reflect the spirit of such laws in their business practices, even though not obligated to abide by the letter of the law.

Guidelines for Practice

When determining your insurance needs and selecting policies...

1. Consider that you may not be totally covered by your employer's insurance or, if you are, that the insurance lawyer assigned to a case will be your employer's lawyer, not your own. You may want to supplement insurance essentially protecting your employer with your own private insurance plan.
2. If you buy your own insurance, make sure your insurance company is solvent and financially secure.
3. Check your insurance company's record of claims payment for fairness and efficiency.
4. Examine your policy's terms and conditions for limitations, including suits for intentional negligence and criminal acts.
5. Consider the insurance plans offered by professional mental health organizations and those that specialize in liability coverage for counseling professionals and mental health organizations.
6. When your insurance needs change, change the coverage on your policy to accommodate them.

When advertising your professional counseling services...

1. The advertisement should conform both in form and in content to lawful state licensing board regulations and ethical

standards published by professional associations, national certifying boards, and state regulatory boards.
2. The advertisement should both be truthful and accurate, and make no unverifiable claims as to quality of service.
3. The advertisement should be reviewed by an attorney experienced in both mass media law and the law of mental health regulations.

When making a contract . . .

1. State your goals, aims, and negotiated ends clearly.
2. State what happens if one party does not abide by the contract.
3. Be aware that contracts can be made verbally or with behaviors that establish a pattern of expectations.

Before signing any contract . . .

1. Read it thoroughly.
2. If you are unclear or uncertain about any of the terms or conditions, express your concerns, and if necessary, seek legal advice and renegotiate the terms.
3. If you are unable to comply with a term or condition of the contract, express your unwillingness to sign under the current terms.
4. Once you have signed a contract, abide by it. If your circumstances materially change, negotiate a change in the agreement.

When a client breaks a contract . . .

1. The failure to pay, or otherwise not to comply, may be consistent with the client's diagnosis or situation. Breaking the contract should be treated as any other treatment situation.
2. If nothing is resolved and you want to pursue payment, give the client notice orally and in writing of your intentions to sue for payment in either civil or small claims court—depending upon the amount in arrears. Remember: If you make a threat to go to court, you may have to make good on it.
3. In deciding whether to sue a client for bad debts, take into account the chances of success. Also consider the costs of attorneys' fees, billable time lost, possible damage to your

reputation, and the possibility of the client's retaliation through a countersuit or ethics violation complaint.
4. If no settlement is reached, make good on your intentions.

To avoid discrimination in the workplace . . .

1. Obtain the synopses of the laws and cases pertaining to job discrimination.
2. Share this material with supervisors and with employees through in-service training and other educational opportunities.
3. Require supervisors to set the example with their own conduct.

As a supervisor or employer addressing sexual harassment . . .

1. Clearly define impermissible sexually related conduct. Establish procedures for investigating and prosecuting complaints and for imposing sanctions.
2. Set the example yourself in both word and in deed.
3. Carry out the stated policies consistently.

To protect your agency, department, or employer from suits based upon vicarious liability . . .

1. Require that all credentials be on file prior to employment.
2. Make a background check of references; if a reference indicates that further investigation for possible past criminal or unethical behavior is required, make the necessary inquiries.
3. Require continuing education for all professional employees based on commonly agreed upon goals and objectives.
4. Make sure all employment policies and procedures are understood and adhered to by all employees.
5. Require a system of peer education and peer review for all professional staff.

When considering using another's copyrighted material . . .

1. To be safest, assume the material falls within the copyright restrictions and cannot be used without express permission

from the copyright owner. Secure such permission prior to using the material.
2. Remember that the primary exceptions from copyright protection are fair use and educational use, which are limited protections.
3. Remember that you are not excused from copyright infringement simply because you are not paid for a particular presentation, lecture, or other program.

If you want copyright protection for your work ...

1. The work must be original and in tangible form.
2. The work must include the insignia © followed by your name and date.
3. To register your work with the U.S. Copyright Office, obtain the necessary materials. (The address of the Copyright Office is noted in the section on Copyright.)
4. When publishing your work, read the publishing contract carefully to determine which party will hold the copyright.

Summary

Counseling is a business. It is, therefore, like any other business and governed by a host of rules and regulations. This monograph introduces these topics in such a way that mental health professionals can immediately apply the major topical sections, the frequently asked questions, and the guidelines for practice as well as the following discussion questions and suggested readings. Mental health professionals—both those in business for themselves and those in private agencies and government departments—should stay abreast of the law and its implications for the mental health industry. Without knowledge of current laws, mental health practitioners are vulnerable to civil and criminal penalties.

Another circumstance that brings mental health professionals headlong into business law is their own rise in professional stature. As counselors and educators rise in professional responsibilities and expertise, they become managers and supervisors of other counselors and educators. The legal knowledge useful for direct mental health practice is not adequate for mental health management. New responsibilities require new knowledge. The business of mental health practice requires legal knowledge formerly reserved for businesspersons and management personnel. Advertising law, insurance law, the sometimes esoteric aspects of federal employment discrimination law (including sexual harassment and pregnancy discrimination), and contract law are but a few of the laws that pose challenges to the mental health professional.

Discussion Questions

1. Why can employers be sued for the wrongful acts of counseling employees? What are the legal theories used to hold employers liable for the torts of their employees? What elements are necessary for departments and other employing agencies to succeed in these lawsuits? How can counseling professionals protect themselves from vicarious employer liability?

2. Most people know what *free speech* means, but what does *commercial free speech* mean? What is the balance that the law tries to strike when allowing counseling professionals to advertise their work while also allowing state licensing boards to regulate some forms of advertising? What kinds of information in advertisements could be construed as false or misleading? What kinds of information are most likely to be considered lawful and useful?

3. Why is copyright protection important for the public? Why is copyright protection important to some counseling professionals? What are the main exceptions against copyright infringement and how might they apply in counseling occupations? What are the three symbols necessary to inform others of the intent to protect original, tangible material copyright? What is the relationship between copyright and plagiarism?

4. Why may agencies and other counseling employers need insurance to protect against business liability as well as insur-

ance to protect against personal liability? What are the elements counseling professionals should look for when choosing an insurance policy?

5. How do contracts act to influence and affect the counseling professions? How many ways might contracts be used in counseling? How can a counseling professional advertently or inadvertently create a contract without benefit of paper or pen? What are the pros and cons of suing a client for late or nonpayment of fees?

6. What situations might give rise to charges of sexual harassment? How might supervisors and employers prevent sexual harassment? What are the steps employees might take when sexually harassed?

7. What is the national policy driving civil rights legislation regarding discrimination in the workplace? What are the most crucial and pressing areas of discrimination for current employers of counselors? How might private mental health centers differ from public agencies in how discrimination cases may arise, how supervisors may prevent them, and how they may be addressed and adjudicated?

8. How can counseling employers keep pace with existing laws related to employment as well as changes and additions to that body of legislation and case law? What are the primary areas of legal vulnerability for your own agency or departments? Where can you find legal information, aids, and materials to eliminate those vulnerabilities?

Suggested Readings

American Association for Counseling and Development. (no date). *Where do you draw the line?* Washington, DC: Author. Pamphlet outlining the definitions and employer responsibilities relative to sexual harassment.

Hopkins, B. R., & Anderson, B. S. (1990). *The counselor and the law* (3rd ed.). Alexandria, VA: American Association for Counseling and Development. Broadly covers several important issues including confidentiality, civil liability, defamation, breach of contract, some criminal actions, and tax considerations.

Lieberman, J. K., & Siedel, G. J. (1985). *Business law and the legal environment.* Washington, DC: Harcourt, Brace, Jovanovich. Thoroughly discusses business law with case examples, illustrations, and analyses.

Margenau, E. A. (Ed.). (1990). *The encyclopedic handbook of private practice.* New York: Gardner Press. Comprehensive essays on most facets of developing and prospering in private practice, including both managerial and legal issues.

Woody, R. H. (1989). *Business success in mental health practice.* San Francisco: Jossey-Bass. Readable discussion of general marketing and business practices as well as legal issues.

References

Age Discrimination and Employment Act of 1975, 42 U.S.C. § 6101 (West 1983 and Supp. 1992).
American Association of Sex Educators, Counselors, and Therapists. (1992). *Contemporary Sexuality, 26*(2), 6.
Americans With Disabilities Act, 42 U.S.C. § 1210 (1990).
Backover, A. (1991). Advertising and counselors: What works? What doesn't? *Guidepost, 34*(4), 11, 20, 41.
Basic Books, Inc. v. Kinko's Graphics Corp., 758 F. Supp. 1522 (S.D.N.Y. 1991).
Bratt v. IBM Corp., 467 N.E.2d 126 (Mass. 1984).
Central Hudson Gas v. Public Service Comm'n., 447 U.S. 557 (1980).
Civil Rights Act of 1964, 42 U.S.C. § 2000e (West 1981).
Civil Rights Reauthorization Act of 1991 (P.L. 102-167, 1991).
Clark, C. S. (1991, October 13). Sexual harassment. *Richmond Times-Dispatch*, pp. F1, F3.
Code of Federal Regulations 29 (C.F.R.) Sections 1630.1 ff (Feb. 28, 1991).
Copyright Act of 1976, 17 U.S.C. § 90 (West 1977).
Cosgrove v. Lawrence, 522 A.2d 483 (N.J. Super. A.D. 1987).
Doe v. Samaritan Counseling Center, 791 P.2d 344 (Alaska, 1990).
Ellison v. Brady, 924 F.2d 872 (1991).
Equal Pay Act of 1963, 29 U.S.C. § 206 (West 1978 and Supp. 1992).

Erikson v. Curtis Investment Co., 432 N.W.2d 199 (Minn. App. 1988).
Family Counseling Service of Clark Co. v. Rust, 462 F. Supp. 74 (1978).
Fenton, J. W., Ruud, W. N., & Kimbell, J. A. (1991). Negligence training suits: A recent entry into the corporate employment negligence arena. *Labor Law Journal, 46,* 351–356.
Friedman, J., & Strickler, G. (1987). *The law of employment discrimination.* Mineola, NY: Foundation Press.
Gibson v. Hummel, 688 S.W.2d 4 (Mo. App. 1985).
Goldberg, S. B. (1991). Hostile environments. *ABA Journal, 77,* 90–92.
Grasso, G. A. (1989). How to keep your clients from suing you. *ABA Journal, 75,* 98, 100.
Gutheil, T. G., & Appelbaum, P. S. (1982). *Clinical handbook of psychiatry and the law.* New York: McGraw-Hill.
Hammar, R. R. (1990). *The church guide to copyright law.* Matthews, NC: Christian Ministry Resources.
Hays, C. L. (1991, May 31). Promotion for detective after settling bias suit. *New York Times,* p. B3.
Hopkins v. Price Waterhouse, 109 S. Ct. 1775 (1989).
Keeton, W. P., Dobbs, D. B., Keeton, R. E., & Owen, D. G. (1984, 1988). *Prosser and Keeton on the law of torts.* St. Paul, MN: West.
Latman, A., Gorman, R., & Ginsburg, J. (1985). *Copyright for the eighties.* Charlottesville, VA: Michie.
Lewin, T. (1991, May 16). Partnership in firm awarded to victim of sex bias. *New York Times,* pp. A1, A20.
Lieberman, J. K., & Siedel, G. J. (1985). *Business law and the legal environment.* Washington, DC: Harcourt, Brace, Jovanovich.
Local 28 of Sheet Metal Workers v. EEOC, 478 U.S. 421 (1986).
Maine harassment law in effect, has no fines. (1991, October 20). *Richmond Times-Dispatch,* p. A4.
Martin Luther King, Jr., Center for Social Change, Inc. v. American Heritage Products, Inc., 508 F. Supp. 324 (N.D. Ga. 1981).
McGowan, S. (1991). Sexual harassment in the workplace. *Guidepost, 34*(7), 1.
McSurely v. McClellan, 753 F.2d 88 (D.C. Cir. 1985).
Meritor Savings Bank v. Vinson, 477 U.S. 77 (1986).

National Association of Social Workers. (1991). Contract clause could boost liability risks. *NASW News, 36*(10), 15.
Nelson, P. L. (1991). Is your insurance company safe? *Guidepost, 34*(5), 4.
New Jersey Statute § 45: 8B-5 (1978).
North Carolina Statutes §§ 90-331-2 (1990).
Peninsula Counseling Center v. Rahm, 719 P.2d 926 (Wash. 1986).
Phillips v. Smalley Maintenance Services, 435 So.2d 705 (Ala. 1983).
Postol, L. P., & Kadue, D. D. (1991). An employer's guide to the Americans With Disabilities Act. *Labor Law Journal, 46,* 323–342.
Pregnancy Discrimination Act, 42 U.S.C.A. 2000e(k) (1981).
Reuschlein, H. G., & Gregory, W. A. (1990). *The law of agency and partnership.* Minneapolis: West.
Robbins, A. C. (1991). The abominable client. *Family Advocate, 13*(4), 21–24.
Robinson v. Jacksonville Shipyards, Inc., 760 F. Supp. 1486 (1991).
Rosenfeld, M. (1991, October 17). Hands-off office guide for men. *Washington Post,* pp. C1–2.
Ross, J. C. (1992). New Civil Rights Act. *ABA Journal, 78,* 85.
Scott, N. (1990, August 26). Pregnancy discrimination is illegal. *Richmond Times-Dispatch,* p. H-13.
Silver, M. (1987). Negligent hiring claims take off. *ABA Journal, 75,* 72–78.
Simmons v. United States, 805 F.2d 1363 (9th Cir. 1986).
Slonaker, W. M., & Wendt, A. C. (1991). Pregnancy discrimination: An empirical analysis of a continuing problem. *Labor Law Journal, 42,* 343–350.
Sonnheim v. State Bd. of Marriage Counselor Examiners, 450 A.2d 1331 (N.J. Super. A.D. 1982).
Tarasoff v. Regents, University of California, 551 P.2d 334 (Cal. 1976).
Ward's Cove Packing Co. v. Atonio, 490 U.S. 642 (1989).
Werner v. Kliewer, 710 P.2d 1250 (Kans. 1985).
Woody, R. H. (1989). *Business success in mental health practice.* San Francisco: Jossey-Bass.
Wygant v. Jackson Bd. of Education, 476 U.S. 267 (1986).

NOTES

NOTES

NOTES